Love & Me

First Printing November 2025

ISBN 978-1-966013-02-0

Published by Sula Too Publishing, Tampa, Florida
Printed in the United States

Love & Me

By
Katrina Blanchett

Thank You

First, I want to thank God for giving me the chance to share my words with the world. I also want to thank my family and extended family who have come into my life along the way to help me get through life's toughest moments and teach me the value of true partnership. I am grateful to each person who has played a vital role in my life, helping me not just to overcome but to survive life's battles, so I didn't fall. They provided me safe spaces to experience unconditional love and endless support.

Forward

Katrina Blanchett has created something both deeply personal and universally relevant — a guide for self-discovery paired with poetry that breathes life into every lesson. This book shares experiences, reflections, and truths that remind us we are never alone in our struggles. Through practical wisdom and poetic expression, readers are invited to pause, reflect, and find strength in unexpected places.

This self-journey is enriched by poems that accompany reflections, conveying emotion, memory, and meaning more effectively than words alone. These poems serve as reminders that growth involves not only thinking differently but also feeling deeply.

As you begin this book, remember you are joining a conversation about wisdom and art. Let the lessons guide you and allow poetry to inspire your spirit. Aside from gaining insight, I hope you feel a renewed sense of possibility after reading these pages to support your inner and outer self-journey.

Dr. Tonya Thomas

Table of Contents

A letter from me …

This journey has come with its share of twists and turns swinging between happiness, sadness, and a creation of love that neither of us knew exist. We took apart the walls we both had changed our ways to ensure we would grow, put away the games where we hotch scotched over people's emotions. He had to keep the motion going to avoid the need to stay in one place.

It sometimes feels like a half-sided dream of promises that we both occasionally drop the ball on, especially when the weight of the world crashes down on us.

Are we pushing each other apart, grasping at straws, or is this a test to see if we can truly move past it? Love is an emotion filled with actions and feelings that can feel like bliss. Some say it shouldn't be so complicated, but life circumstances often interfere with the plans we want to make. It can feel like a fairy tale, but reality is harsh and hard to connect with. Seeing the person you have an unexplainable desire for turn away, walk out the door, and move on with life can be devastating. Explaining that pain to someone can drive you insane because no one can understand the hold of a soul shared by two people—if one walks away, the other feels like they are slowly dying inside. Words or actions from anyone else can't fill that deep void or heal that intense, unspoken war.

During this time, you feel you're doing what's best, and that time will heal and get less and less. But what you have in him and her nobody else can possess because what you thought was supposed to be a short time, not a long time, was set up to last an eternity. You can tell yourself lies and sell the world pipe dreams, but who are you being honest with? Definitely not yourself. Live outside of fear, live outside of what society thinks, live for yourself, and follow what truly brings happiness. We are on borrowed time. Each day that passes, we run out of time more and more. If you want something different, you have to come out of your comfort zone and open your eyes. Show love out loud and express it openly for the world to see. Keeping that type of limited edition a secret is doing a disservice to yourself, knowing that the truth is love happens when you least expect it, no matter how much you guard your heart and try to protect it. Some things are the assignment in your life that you can't reject, neglect, or even move past, but learn to accept it and find a solution to handle it for the betterment of each other's mental health.

Type of Love

The kind of love I need
is one that doesn't require weapons
but the strength to keep my mind healthy

When I fall short
this love gives me the strength
to get through that day
just a little longer

It's the kind that, in silence
fills the room with unspoken chatter
and can make us burst out laughing
as if a joke was told out loud

It's the kind that
when I look into your eyes
time freezes because

I'm traveling through our love patterns
the greatest love of all

It's the kind I feel
even when I want to
run away from the world
but not having you in it
would be a crime

You're the officer
who would lock me up
and throw away the key
because you don't want
anyone else to experience
the grace of my love

This love is a magical
an unconventional gift

that can't be bought with riches
because it's not for sale

It's the joy of having enough between us
enough just to be together

The love I seek and find wealth in
isn't measured by price tags or money
It's unconditional

Love that grows and defines itself over time
with no expiration date

The kind where you have
"just because thoughts"
as simple as walking
into a place and saying
"This reminds me of my baby,"

and I can't wait to see
the smile on their faces
as they enjoy the gestures of your picking

The kind where a simple foot or back rub
is like planting endless kisses that you
embrace as each motion moves around your
body

It's the kind where
you just want to bask in old feelings
and a never-ending love story
with endless hugs and cuddles

The safest place is in your arms
with whispers of "I love you" in my ear
before bed or during early morning wakeups

It's the kind that makes you grab your chest
and feel like you might have a heart attack
because the thought of not being a part of
your world anymore makes no sense

Existing within the walls of our love
which is only for two
is the only thing that makes my heart pump

Yeah, this is the kind of love I crave
and want in this lifetime and beyond.

Heart

I gave you my heart without hesitation

At first, I had many doubts
about who you really were
but I let the walls fall down
brick by brick, just to let you in
something I usually never do

I'm usually the type to complain
that love hardly ever felt real in my eyes
I could have gone on
without feeling any of this

What they don't tell you is
when you let your defenses down and
love with an open heart

Man, it can leave you vulnerable enough
to believe that fairy tales do come true
and all that magic you saw as a kid
can happen in real life

But it's halfway right

love will sometimes come back
to bite and can be unfair
making you want to retreat to the safe
rough edges of your old guarded self
because the soft, clingy
wanting-to-shower-in-love-overflow-side
leaves you lonely
fighting back tears
over a dead-end love
with a man you truly want
but just seems like it won't happen

So your heart bleeds and pushes you back
into the shell of thinking
no man will ever take you back there

Keep that in the books, because this kind of
love will leave you with thorns all around
protecting you from being torn apart
by disappointments and broken promises
tricking you into believing
it could be a happy ending
when, in reality
we couldn't even finish the rough draft.

Lock n key

With this key, I give you the complete part of me
the windows of my heart to open and
never depart from the depths of this love we
share that makes our souls glow
leaving an effect on everything
that comes our way

You are my first love
and I want you to be my last

God placed us on this path to finally meet
to bring out the greatest parts
from the start with no ending

To take us out of comfort and
step into our better halves

Even in the battles of loving you
I would still choose you
just like that old favorite dress
that never goes out of season

Just like the sand that stuck to the glue
with our hands pressed together
as lifetime imprints
beyond physical attachments

Just wait, you will see

God's timing is the perfect set of keys
to unlock all our dreams
the foundation of our reality
the most treasured keepsake
of this undeniable love

unfolding as it is meant to be
creating a happy fit
where peaceful lives seem best
for you and me.

Skin

I want to be wherever you are
but you keep me at a distance
letting me in only so far

I want to be your safe space
with a time capsule of memories
paused in place

I want to be able to love you healthily
nothing like you've experienced

So, it's a personalized act
that can't be replaced or jacked

I want to create the peaceful space
that gives you inspiration
to move about in your day
to position you to feel like I'm still near

Within us, you don't have to be afraid
and you hear my voice loud and clear

You being you is more than enough
I'm always going to show up.

Fit

Where do I fit in this life?
Sometimes it feels like
I'm looking at a portrait
that doesn't have my face
or like I'm in a movie theater
watching clips of a life happening
I didn't buy a ticket for

I'm in the audience in dead silence
looking around
and there is no one else in the crowd

It's like looking in a mirror of the future
but all you hear
is the loud sounds of the past
trying to pull you back
keeping you trapped

in a dark place of motivation
of no love

Survival kicks in to just crawl back
look deep within, and ask
Who do I want to be?

Not a life of misery or stagnation of no hope
drowning in fears of love
not happening for me

Watching others live their dreams and
carry out their plans
plays mental tricks on you

Your mind is stuck looking at time passing
some aspects of life try to align
while others are like the blind leading the
blind.

Can you? Will you?

Can you love me despite my fears?
When anxiety kicks in
Will you let me drown in my sorrow?

In my tears
Will you be patient as I struggle mentally
diving deep into my thoughts and
unable to find a peaceful place
to help my heart regain its steady rhythm?

Will you fight for me
when I show signs of unease and
put us in an uncomfortable space?

Can you support
all my dreams and aspirations

even if they seem strange
and are just rambling thoughts
scattered everywhere?

Can you. Will you fight for me
every day to show that your love
wasn't a phase or something
I can easily erase or be replaced
as if our love could be lost without a trace?

I just need you to know
when my insecurities show up

Will you be my saving grace
to help me keep fighting for another day
or will you abandon me
to pick up the pieces
of my long history of disappointments
spiraling out of control?

Will you, can you
keep showing up and fighting
because I mean too much
for you to just give up?

Will you, can you
always be willing
to be the words
as I am the pen,
to write the story
that never ends?

Behind her eyes

Behind those eyes is a woman
who longs to be loved
like what you read in books
where she is that man's missing piece

Lies are never told to her
and tears of joy are
the only ones that grace her face

The pain of past wounds
no longer drains her
instead, her wildest dreams
are coming true
as she acts them out in reality
to put herself in a winning seat

All the doubt and guilt no longer consume
her
no longer holding her in a death grip
always avoiding being cut at the tip

and feeling the need to play fair
or wave the white flag
in friendships and entanglements
because they no longer
serve her purpose moving forward

It's a story still being written
with some bumps and bruises along the way

It's a mother who
only wants to see her kids succeed
and be successful on their own

She is a woman of many talents
able to tap into any of them
to make it happen

It's a heart that sometimes doesn't sleep
or needs mental breaks
from the world to stay grounded

She is a woman who smiles outwardly
even when inside
her inner walls are crumbling
because she has to remember
to fix her own crown

She is a woman
who knows she has superpowers
that God gifted her to shine a light
and help others be bright
even if she sometimes dims her own
to let others sit and
fit where time has expired
and they can no longer
join the table of happiness

A woman whose intentions matter
and words are empty

without actions behind them

She needs and wants alignment
with what has her name on it
something perfectly designed
with her in mind
because nothing else will fit

Sadness, pain, doubt
and even fear lie behind those beautiful eyes
often covered up with
pretending to be happy and at peace

But inside, she is distraught
trying to make sense of the world around her
so she doesn't become
another broken woman
who gives up in defeat

She doesn't allow the world around her
to break her or make her feel
like she will never be good enough

Yet she learns that her value is defined
by who and what she truly wants to be

She sets own standards
for how she wants others to see her
not what they want her to be
Her eyes, looking back at herself
are the only ones that truly matter.

Testimonial One

I In 2021, at age 34, I finally had an encounter with what I never knew would turn into real unconditional love, with tests from all angles and turns. I was always easy-going and followed the beat to my own drum. I never tried to get too attached to anyone or anything. Out of self-protection to avoid getting hurt in love and relationships.

The less I cared, the easier it was to move on, which is how I felt. Well, boy, I was wrong. I end up meeting this perfect, imperfect man who changed my life on many levels and views forever.

As for love, and how true unconditional love can bring many challenges, you see, no matter how right and perfect you love someone and how the pieces fit into the puzzle of your story, there is always a twist that comes with it. If you're not careful, a person won't truly be able to see you as they need to in order to love you for who you are.

For things to thrive and survive, it takes accountability and open, uncut honesty not taking each other to heart when emotions run high and tempers are flaring. When the tempers are at a no-man's level of comeback, that is when you truly see if the person sees you as unconditionally as you see them. But sadly, that's not always the case; you're left feeling unseen, unheard— all because, no matter what, they will never truly be able to see you as they need to.

Couldn't see

You couldn't see me, even though
I was the brightest light in the dark room

I was the motivation
When it was all messy and doomed

I was the prayer that God answered
When he listened to my cries

While my heart is pounding and broken
It's the decisions made with no remorse

It's the broken cycles of deception
That's fully run its course

At one point, I wanted nothing more
than to be connected past
the human touch of flesh
I wanted the innermost and deepest touch

As Eve's to Adam's rib

The amount of weight
that is carried to the depths
of that type of intimacy
births the fear of walking in self-truths
of who you are within

It blinds you to see
the worth of the woman
who stands before you

Your own lack of value is the mirror
You are trying to see her through
A broken lens and in unhealed ways

All she ever wanted was
for you to see her naked
Unafraid to love the ugly you

But you couldn't see her.

Me

What makes me, me?
 is the questions asked

Is it the 99 versions of myself
 I'm always trying to please?

Is it the missing love or spirit
I'm trying to fight off
because I seem to want it at any cost?

Am I in denial that I'm quite fragile
and sometimes just want to be held
to feel safe, not just exist in place?

Who am I?
Runs through my mind
and tries to understand myself

At times understanding myself
drives me insane

What do I want?
I haven't sought it

It's like endless pitter-patter
My soul feels shattered
I look in the mirror
and see a woman of essence and resilience

With battles and all odds against her
she stands tall
because she has little gentlemen
and protecting them
is her greatest testimony

That makes her the greatest mommy
in this life of sin

I will never pretend
when given a helping hand
to those I love the most

The genuine care I give
will always make anyone feel like
they can fly through the skies
through thunderstorms
and remain unharmed

Who am I?
The most unique human being
that God took His time with
sketching and tracing every detail

down to the dimple
on the left side of my face

Who am I?
There are so many answers
to what seems like a simple question
To figure out who I truly am
I need unlimited time

Unconditional love
feeds my mind
when I feel no grace from above
guidance, when I go astray
I just begin to get on my knees and
pray to the Father and the Son
who will always be my saving grace.

Self

Self
the Brightest Light in the Darkest Room
the woman you can't put on a shelf

She's not a wait-for-later type
but the kind who will pour out and fill your
cup

She provides overflowing love and
knows what you need
as if it's a second instinct
fulfilling all your dreams

She is the woman
who goes after what she wants
her hustle game is strong

She's always making sure
her family eats and has a plan

for all seasons to come

You can count on her
to think outside the box
and turn all your fairy tales into reality

Her beauty isn't only surface deep
her inner beauty guides her
revealing what's deep inside her
making anything before her a blur

Besides her prosperity and joy
she's a woman with a heart
of gold and pure intentions

Heck, she might even
be considered a limited edition.

Gone

I didn't realize how much I needed you
 until you were no longer
part of my daily life

This kind of pain, they say
eases and goes away over time
but each passing day without you
makes my heart chip away more

I crave you—
like the day craves sunlight
like the moon that shines at night
Without these things
the world would be
completely dark and unbright

It's crazy that your mind says let go
but my heart is stronger
It beats with purpose
every time your image appears
and the butterflies you learned about
when you were younger start to flutter again

The sound of your voice
is the sweetest melody
and my favorite thing to hear

I imagine you here
or hear that knock at the door
to wipe away all the fear
and pain I'm fighting.

We made sense
life made sense

Now it's just blurred
and existing has become the new norm

Life can change in a blink

If only time could pause
and I could redo it all
I would still choose you
without a second thought.

Wait

Cry it out, scream it out, yell
whatever makes the soul shout
 to release this banging and the agony
of misleading words

Everything that was said
are the thoughts replaying in my head
the burning of a ghost's soul
that went cold

Longing for a loving embrace
to warm the place that once
was meant not to be erased
 now an empty space with clarity to learn
how to adjust and be more selective
 about whom I let into my inner energy

To avoid past mistakes circling around
just to end up in the same place
with no more regrets, doubts, and fears.

Unlimited possibilities
are all I hear
loud as day

I'm saving you day by day
Lean on my understanding
to pave the way

Hold on to my voice,
be still
and peace I will reveal.

Screams

Screaming out loud
as my hands grip my hair
I pour out the thoughts that plague my mind

If only people understood the thoughts
that go on in my head some days
feeling empty, lost, and afraid to be alone
while on other days
feeling joy and optimism
about what could be

I don't want to become just another lost soul
placed on a shelf like an unknown souvenir

Tired of overpouring, nearly empty
from a lack of empathy
my heart feels manipulated
like a broken string
on her favorite violin

Depression runs deep
I just want to be set free
to find love that truly finds and chooses me

I wonder what the recipe is
for having someone else
not just me again

Thoughts – Is it them or just me?

Dead End

I have a history and a past
but they don't define me

Even if you put me on blast
and tell all my dirty secrets
I don't care because it won't stick

It's my past and doesn't determine my future
only learned lessons
that keep people guessing

How did she
oh no, it couldn't be
I hate that girl
even for what I can't see

She doesn't deserve anything but misery

I'm ruining any chance of happiness

It won't exist if I play my hand
at destroying her and that man

Then I would be able to sit in the corner
and laugh as my plans come together
like dominoes, all falling into place

I'm enjoying the show
I just know it will break them for-sho
It won't be a chance
in hell their love will stick

He will desert her
like a broken broom to a stick
leaving her broken again
just like all the other men

who only wanted to give a quick thrill
with nothing real

Pushing her further away
she can't even begin to heal
I want her to feel

all the hurt and pain as I do
so we can always
remain the same two broken women
with deadly spirits
trapped in unhealthy feelings.

Second Testimony

In March 2025, I was 17 weeks pregnant at age 37, just two weeks away from turning 38. I experienced a major shift in my life that would change me forever. What should have been a routine checkup for my baby turned into a nightmare when I learned that my precious little girl's heart had stopped beating. I remember hearing the words come out of the doctor's mouth: "I'm so sorry," but the words didn't fully register in my mind what she was truly saying. I kept asking myself how, why, and what—this couldn't be happening to me. I was pleading, "God, please no," but deep down I knew it was true. In that split second, I had to decide how to handle the passing of my daughter. I had to go to the hospital to deliver her, even though I still had five months to go. The heartbreak of that thought shattered me into a million pieces. At the same time, I wondered how I could tell my kids that their sister was gone and that the excitement of welcoming a girl into our home was no longer real. As I prepared for this nightmare, I kept thinking that at some point I would wake up or realize it was just a bad dream. But as they began preparing me for delivery—something I had experience doing with my three other living children—I started sobbing with deep wails because the questions of "why" and "how" were tearing at my soul. I wished so badly that this wasn't my reality. Nine hours of labor later, Marley was born—an eternal part of my life and a source of inspiration for the woman I've become. She is the reason I strive to be the best version of myself, so in heaven she can have a mother she's proud of, and here on earth, her brothers can remember her. Losing my baby brought many challenges and twists, especially since I bled out three days later due to the hospital not fully checking for all the placenta. The heartbreak of losing her also took a toll on my mental and emotional well-being. But I kept pushing forward because I trusted that there was a purpose behind her passing. Even though I lost many relationships during this grieving process, it also created unbreakable bonds with those whom the Lord sent to support me.

Marley

4 months
16 weeks
1,742 minutes
I carried you in my womb
and during that time
our heartbeats matched

I knew you would bring out the best in me
I knew that God was blessing me with you,
even if it was for a short time

I will still keep my promise to you
I'm grateful that my family grew
from three to four

With that
my life gained
much more meaning and purpose
to be the greatest mother of a lifetime

to my earth babies
as well as my angel girl.

Blissful

A blissful feeling that is unexplainable
makes the hairs on your arms stand up

The knots you feel in your stomach are
butterflies
and the smile on your face
keeps your cheeks stuck in place

No matter what you do, you can't erase
the sensation of this spiritual place
where you are finally at peace

Here, love and forgiveness reside
and fear no longer consumes you
instead, goals and dreams
are slowly being met.

To be able to walk through
all the doors ahead of you

Don't give up this is only a test
Keep going
face all opposition
by telling the devil to rest
and look to God for the tools
to work through endless obstacles

With your eyes closed
both hands pray to God
for the release of all your sins

Give the strength
that no human can provide
to put you back together
in the only way God's presence can.

Don't Tell Me

Don't tell me
that I'm okay
just because I look
like I can carry all this weight.

Don't tell me
that if it were you
you would do it differently.

Don't tell me
that your happiness is my only safe space.

Don't tell me
that you are at peace knowing
you erase everything

that represents me in you
and that joy now lives within you

Don't tell me
I don't cross your mind when you are lying
in bed at night or battling your inner
thoughts.

Don't tell me
that we still have time;
just let you figure it out.

Don't tell me
that love will always be
knocking at each other's door and
that it's unconditional,
but we can show it.

Don't tell me
I'm the right one or what your soul needs
when you're out here just selling dreams.

Just stop pulling at all the strings of my
heart — it's not like a violin that
you can just replace the string
because a connected string popped
Just stop telling me anything
and be your real self

Don't tell me
I don't know how to approach you
so I never did

Don't tell me
that the death happened between us
don't carry that heavily;
that running is all you do

because sleep can find you
or your health

Don't claim
that because your eyes close
it's better for your mental health
and sleeping is easy
as long as you can lie in a bed
Nah, because the reality is
you live in your head

Don't tell me
your anxiety and insecurity
aren't showing up where a pill won't help

Don't say
you've got it right
just because I'm out of sight

Don't tell me
your life is blessed but your soul is empty
with nothing left

Just don't tell me
because you'd rather keep lying
instead of looking in the mirror of self

I want you to just stop telling me.

Katrina Blanchett

I'm a mother of four who has experienced love, heartbreak, and growth, becoming the best version of myself. I feel like God has a purpose for me to share my words with the world and let my obstacles become my greatest strengths, a testimony. "See you later, Myy butterflies"

Order Multiple Copies Today
Share the Sweetness: Turn Lemons into Gifts

Become a Catalyst for Change
This book is the perfect gift for:
A young woman starting a new chapter.

- A friend going through a difficult time or breakup.
- A single mom striving for independence.
- Anyone who needs a reminder of their inner strength and purpose.

"It was truly amazing how she uses the highs and lows from her own life experiences, inspired by God, to inspire other young ladies to take the lemons dealt to them in their lives to make lemonade. I am so very proud of you sweetheart."
— Kay Francis Long

Your mission is simple: Buy a copy for yourself and buy a copy (or three!) to pass on. **Share the light** and help another woman turn her lemons into refreshing lemonade.**www.katrinakares4u.com**

Support Myy Little Butterflies

www.katrinakares4u.com

HELLO "MYY LITTLE BUTTERFLIES"

What's holding you back from spreading your wings?

Every small act of courage—every decision to lift your chin and fly—creates ripples of inspiration in the world. In this book, you've been provided with the tools, stories, and unwavering belief to begin your own transformation. Now, it's time to fully embrace the magnificent journey ahead.

Be the inspiration. Be the change. Be a butterfly.

Continue your flight! Visit our merchandise site for gifts designed to remind you of the beauty in your transformation, inspire courage, and encourage you to **spread your wings and fly.**

Find your inspiration:
www.KatrinaKares4U.com
Why? Because Katrina Kares 4 You!